ALL THE BUILDINGS* IN LOS ANGELES

*THAT I'VE DRAWN SO FAR
BY JAMES GULLIVER HANCOCK

UNIVERSE

INTRODUCTION

JAMES GULLIVER HANCOCK

Los Angeles is a huge, sprawling beast encrusted with hidden gems, just like a monster in a Hollywood movie. When I first arrived, I had an overwhelming sense of not being welcome. Landing in the heat of LAX on my own at twenty years old, I was instantly hit with the feeling that this place is not designed for humans. I don't think I left my motel near the airport for days, surviving on Pop-Tarts® and tea. The sidewalks outside were seemingly infinite. The heat was intense and dry. Through my young eyes even the 7-Eleven across the road looked like a movie cliche hangout for some shady bad guys. The huge six-lane streets weren't designed to be crossed. Walking in LA seemed futile; I was daunted by the concrete distances in front of me. The only other time I had felt that feeling of urban isolation was in Moscow, where the architecture seemed to be designed to make you feel insignificant. It was like someone took a Brutalist architect's nightmare and flattened it into two dimensions, hiding anything of interest behind closed doors. Little did I know there were amazing things to be discovered.

When I was a child, we had been to Los Angeles on a typical California road trip. We had all the family fun: Disneyland, road trip up the coast, pancakes in diners, hamburgers in the Hard Rock Cafe, and gentle earthquakes rocking us to sleep. It was a fantasy land; but as typically happens on a diet of sugary experiences, it left me unsatisfied and as though I'd only skimmed the surface. This wasn't the real LA either—it still remained hidden.

When I returned to LA later with my girlfriend (now wife) and we set up a life there, the place really blossomed for me. In three years I found an amazing family of friends and places I loved around the city. I scratched below the surface and uncovered an incredible creative community and began the early days of a career in illustration.

(ALL THE CARS IN LOS ANGELES)

Nothing I discovered in LA was by accident though. You can't just walk around and stumble on something. I love to walk and bicycle in cities and so it was really hard for me to find my place in LA. I found that nothing looks amazing on the surface and I really had to rely on local knowledge and tips to find a place for myself. More than any other city I know, it requires a conscious effort to join places together, to talk with people about places they have been, to build your own version of the city and make it your own. In LA you can't rely on the city taking your hand and showing you a good time—you have to keep your eyes peeled and make a personal map of the place.

Like all my experiences of cities, drawing played a big role. One of the first things I did was draw cars. I'd always used drawing to overcome a fear of place when I was traveling and it seemed natural to draw the dominant object of the city. LA is covered in cars and most of our expriences involved the cars we were in. I started to draw the cars I saw around me, the cars I was in, my friends' cars. I became a car chaser, looking for interesting cars. I remember finding a DeLorean on a street in Silver Lake and getting excited (those childhood film-set dreams were still hiding there). Collecting these drawings was theraputic in a way, and it made the intense experience of driving everywhere a personal project that became fun. Drawing is funny like that; how it can take the everyday and make it special and intriguing not only to yourself but to others. I started to relate my daily experience to drawing cars. I utilized my personal leanings toward obsession to draw constantly. I eventually compiled all these drawings into this print on the previous page.

As I integrated more, the architecture in LA soon came to fascinate me as well. I began to understand the way the streets worked and how amazing things could be in a building with absolutely no coding as to what was inside. I remember finding a huge model train set inside what was basically a big gray concrete box. As the insides of buildings started to reveal themselves, I also became interested in their outsides.

I learned about the modernist architects taking to the space, and the potential to build new ideas about what a home could be. The post-World War 2 case study houses where new fabrication techniques where developed and whole new ways of doing things were discovered. The mishmash of Mexican and European constructions was interesting and the amazing art deco and similarly styled civic and theater buildings that had ghosts of Charlie Chaplin and others walking around them. Los Angeles held such promise for creative expression, I started to find it exciting; the potential is huge and so many amazing people have taken advantage of the city's space and freedom.

The climate-driven architecture also felt somehow familiar to my Australian childhood, with eucalyptus trees hanging over the Eames house and low-slung verandas keeping out the sun. Gradually LA became home, and it happened through drawing. I encourage you to get out into the surroundings of a place you like and observe and draw the things around you in an effort to more fully integrate yourself into the environment. You might notice a house you've never seen before, or a street that hides a row of brightly colored houses. There are hidden gems in every city and drawing is a good way to make yourself stop and look at them.

Los Angeles is an incredible place, but I would encourage you to explore with some purpose. Don't wander aimlessly; go with a vision of what you want to discover. You can't help but love the house and garden oasis at the Eames house but driving there might be a nightmare. Nothing comes easy in LA; you need to traverse it consciously. Use this book to find some fascinating architecture and wander this sprawling city on the hunt for beauty between the concrete cracks, and always try and stop and draw the little gems you find for yourself, building a map of the place of your very own.

ROSE BOWL

AKA SPIEKER FIELD

OPENED IN 192~

Rose Bowl

GAMBLE HOUSE

4 WESTMORELAND PLACE, PASADENA

AN AMERICAN ARTS & CRAFTS MASTERPIECE ORIGINALLY BUILT AS A PRIVATE

WINTER RESIDENCE FOR DAVID & MARY GAMBLE

DOWNTOWN LA

UNION STATION

BUILT IN 1939

**555
WEST TEMPLE ST.**

CATHEDRAL OF
OUR LADY OF
THE ANGELS
AKA **C.O.L.A.**

CHINATOWN
CENTRAL
PLAZA

943
NORTH BROADWAY

IT IS FEATURED ON THE L.A.P.D BADGES

200 NORTH SPRING STREET

CITY HALL

COMPLETED 1928

THE CONCRETE USED IN CONSTRUCTION WAS SOURCED FROM CALIFORNIA'S 58 COUNTIES AND WATER FROM ITS 21 HISTORICAL MISSIONS

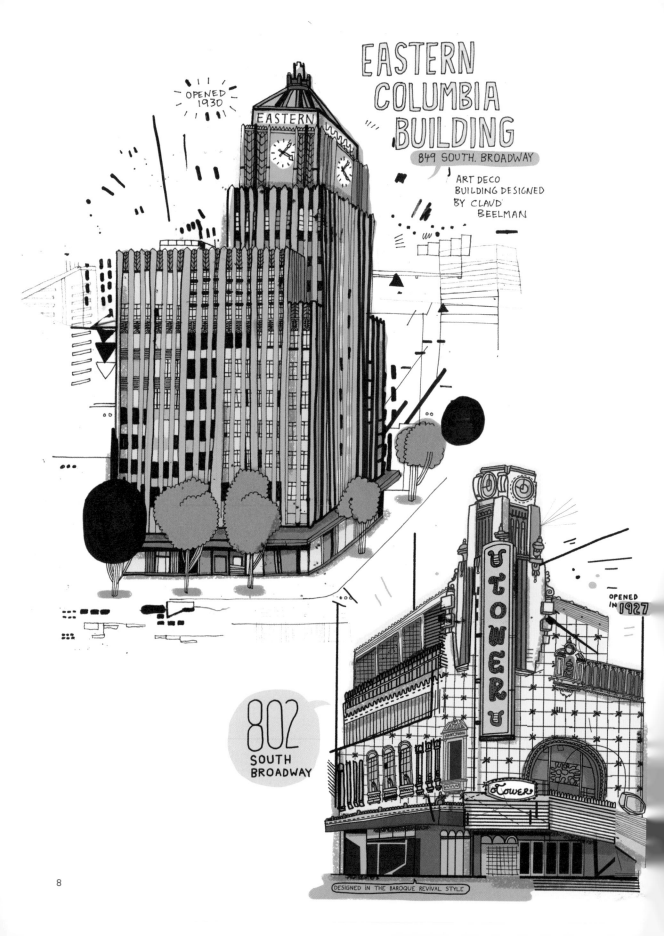

EASTERN COLUMBIA BUILDING

849 SOUTH. BROADWAY

OPENED 1930

EASTERN

ART DECO BUILDING DESIGNED BY CLAUD BEELMAN

802 SOUTH BROADWAY

TOWER

TOWER

OPENED IN 1927

DESIGNED IN THE BAROQUE REVIVAL STYLE

202 WEST 1ST ST

DESIGNED BY GORDON B. KAUFMANN
WON A GOLD MEDAL AT THE PARIS EXPOSITION IN 1937

HERALD EXAMINER BUILDING

146 W. 11TH ST.

DESIGNED IN THE MISSION REVIVAL STYLE
COMPLETED IN 1914

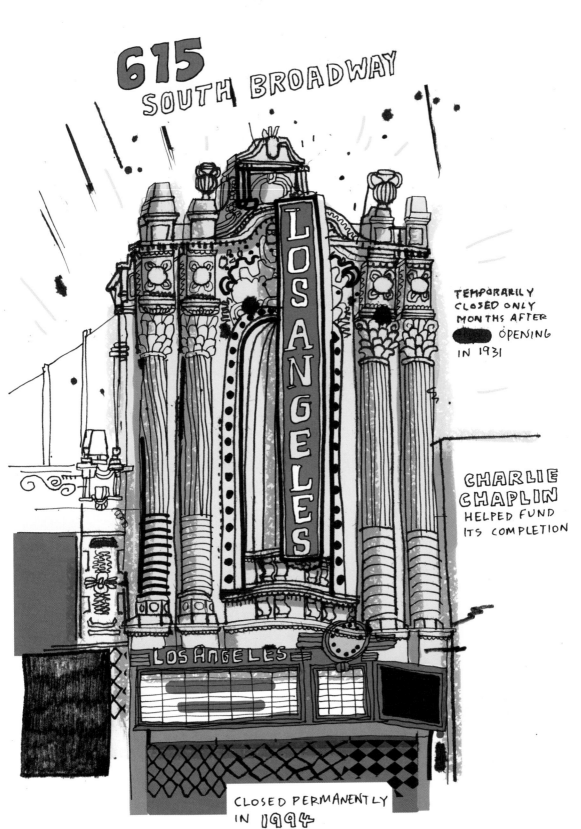

615 SOUTH BROADWAY

TEMPORARILY CLOSED ONLY MONTHS AFTER ⬤ OPENING IN 1931

CHARLIE CHAPLIN HELPED FUND ITS COMPLETION

CLOSED PERMANENTLY IN 1994

A 1,018 FOOT SKYSCRAPER AT **633** WEST 5TH. ST DOWNTOWN L.A.

PARK PLAZA HOTEL
607 PARK VIEW ST
NOW THE MACARTHUR

CREATED BY ART DECO ARCHITECT CLAUD BEELM.

929 SOUTH BROADWAY DOWNTOWN LA

UNITED ARTISTS

HELLO LA

UNIVERSITY PARK

NATURAL HISTORY MUSEUM

ECHO PARK

CARROLL AVE

SHAKESPEARE BRIDGE

BUILT IN 1926
RE-BUILT IN 1998
AFTER AN EARTHQUAKE

LOS FELIZ

GRIFFITH OBSERVATORY

3,015 ACRES OF LAND SURROUNDING THE OBSERVATORY WAS DONATED BY GRIFFITH J. GRIFFITH IN 1896

JAMES DEAN SCRAMBLED AROUND HERE IN REBEL WITHOUT A CAUSE

ENNIS HOUSE

DESIGNED BY FRANK LLOYD WRIGHT AND FEATURED IN THE FILM BLADE RUNNER

Since 1934

SKY

NOR

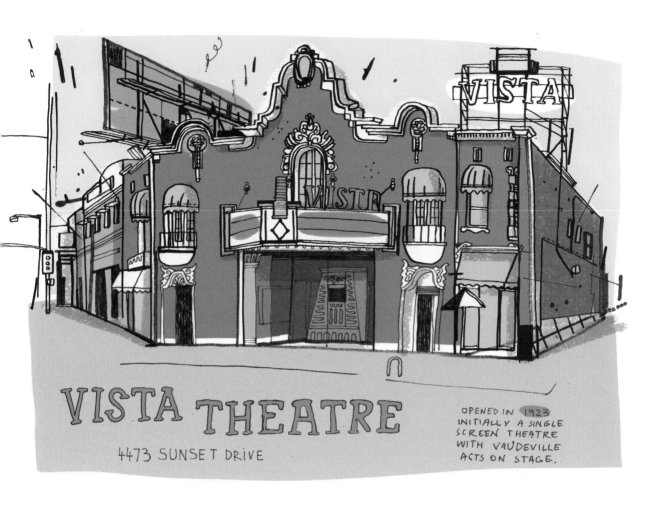

VISTA THEATRE

4473 SUNSET DRIVE

OPENED IN 1923 INITIALLY A SINGLE SCREEN THEATRE WITH VAUDEVILLE ACTS ON STAGE.

MONT AVENUE

4427 SUNSET BLVD.

ESTABLISHED IN 1961 BY RAY BUHEN

EAST HOLLYWOOD

822 MARIPOSA AVENUE

HOLLYHOCK HOUSE
BUILT 1919-1921

ORIGINALLY A PRIVATE RESIDENCE FOR OIL HEIRESS ALINE BARNSDALL.

DESIGNED BY
FRANK LLOYD WRIGHT

720 NORTH VIRGIL AVENUE

LA

720 #4

WINE

THE HIGGINS-VERBECK HOUSE
CUT IN HALF & MOVED FROM
ITS ORIGINAL SITE AT 2619 WILSHIRE

637 LUCERNE SOUTH BLVD

5515
MELROSE
AVENUE

Paramount Pictures

250-236
NORTH LARCHMONT BLVD.

NOAH'S BAGELS

Kika

CELEBRITY CENTRE
5930 FRANKLIN AVE.

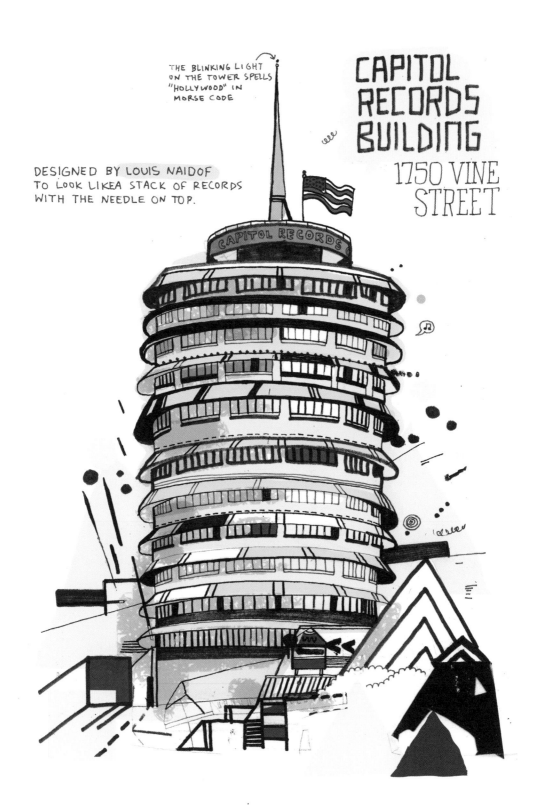

THE BLINKING LIGHT ON THE TOWER SPELLS "HOLLYWOOD" IN MORSE CODE

DESIGNED BY LOUIS NAIDOF TO LOOK LIKE A STACK OF RECORDS WITH THE NEEDLE ON TOP.

CAPITOL RECORDS BUILDING 1750 VINE STREET

CAPITOL RECORDS

A PRIVATE CLUB
FOR MEMBERS AND
THEIR GUESTS.

THE MAGIC CASTLE

7001 FRANKLIN AVENUE

1749
NORTH LA BREA AVE.

WOMAN'S CLUB of HOLLYWOOD

825 NORTH LA BREA AVE.

7000 HOLLYWOOD BLVD.

Canter's Deli

OPENED IN 1931 IN BOYLE HEIGHTS, MOVED TO 419 NORTH FAIRFAX AVE. IN 1953 TO FOLLOW THE MOVEMENT OF THE JEWISH POPULATION AT THE TIME.

WEST HOLLYWOOD

8100 MELROSE

OPENED
IN 1929
AS A PRIVATE RESIDENCE
APARTMENT COMPLEX.
IT WAS CONVERTED
INTO A HOTEL IN 1931.

8221
SUNSET BOULEVARD

Chateau
Marmont
Hotel

SUNSET BLVD.

SAN VICENTE → LARRABEE

SUNSET BLVD.

8484 WILSHIRE BLVD

BEVERLY
HILLS

BEVERLY
HILLS
CITY
HALL

470 NORTH LA CIENEGA BLVD.

OPENED IN 1957
DESIGNED BY ARMET & DAVIS
TO LOOK LIKE AN
AUTOMOBILE SHOW
ROOM.

427 NORTH CRESCENT DR.

NORTH
RODEO
DRIVE

SUN VALLEY

9457 SAN FERNANDO ROAD

VAN NUYS

15212 VALERIO

UNIVERSAL CITY

4824 VINELAND AVENUE

THE J. PAUL GETTY MUSEUM
AKA **THE GETTY CENTER**
1200 GETTY CENTER DR.

OPENED 1997
DESIGNED BY RICHARD M

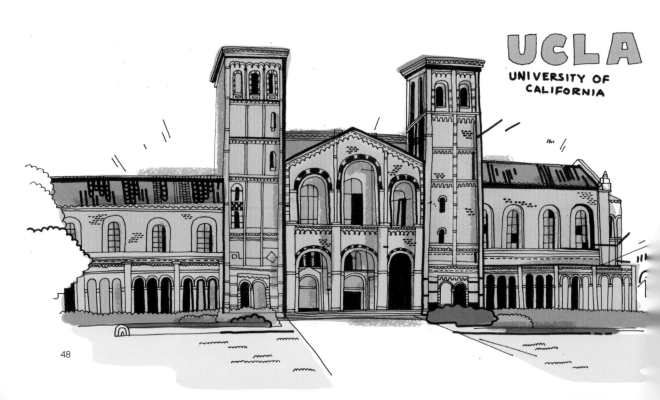

UCLA
UNIVERSITY OF CALIFORNIA

3007 SANTA MONICA BOULEVARD

FORMULAIC APARTMENT BUILDINGS FROM THE '50s AND '60s USUALLY BOXY STUCCO DESIGNS WITH PARKING UNDERNEATH

1138 EUCLID STREET

A CLASSIC EXAMPLE OF **DINGBAT** ARCHITECTURE

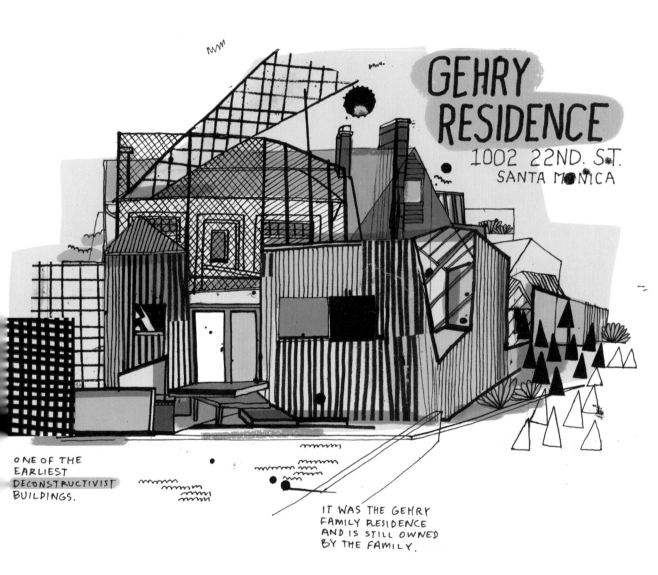

GEHRY RESIDENCE
1002 22ND. ST.
SANTA MONICA

ONE OF THE
EARLIEST
DECONSTRUCTIVIST
BUILDINGS.

IT WAS THE GEHRY
FAMILY RESIDENCE
AND IS STILL OWNED
BY THE FAMILY.

CASE STUDY HOUSE #8
THE EAMES HOUSE
203 NORTH CHAUTAUQUA BLVD.

340 MAIN STREET

THE
BINOCULARS
BUILDING
BY FRANK GEHRY FOR ADVERTISING AGENCY CHIAT/DAY

INCORPORATES
CLAES OLDENBURG'S
GIANT BINOCULARS

330—328
INDIANA AVE.
VENICE

ONCE DENNIS HOPPER'S
COMPOUND, DESIGNED
BY BRIAN MURPHY,

WITH SOME BUILDINGS
ON THE PROPERTY
DESIGNED BY FRANK GEHRY.

SANTA MONICA PIER

OVER 100 YEARS OLD

SANTA MONICA
★ YACHT HARBOR ★
SPORT FISHING ★ BOATI
Cafes

NORTON HOUSE

BY FRANK GEHRY

2509 OCEAN FRONT WALK, VENICE

VENICE CANALS

4616 DUNDEE DR.

LOVELL
BEACH HOUSE

DESIGNED &
BUILT BY
RICHARD
NEUTRA
1927-29

POINT FERMIN

LIGHT HOUSE

BUILT IN 1874 WITH LUMBER FROM CALIFORNIAN REDWOODS

broiler
Bob's
BIG BOY
ORIGINAL
DOUBLE DECK
HAMBURGER
7447 FIRESTONE BLVD.

10207
LAKEWOOD BLVD.

15¢

McDonald's
HAMBURGERS
We have sold over 1 MILLION

McDonald's

THE OLDEST OPERATING
McDONALD'S RESTAURANT

LA VERNE
UNITED METHODIST CHURCH
3205 D STREET

THE CHURCH
FROM THE MOVIE
THE GRADUATE

SAN
GABRIEL
MISSION

3319 ISABEL DR.

GLASSEL PARK

ALTADENA

1675 EAST ALTADENA DRIVE

THE WALSH HOUSE FROM
BEVERLY HILLS 90210

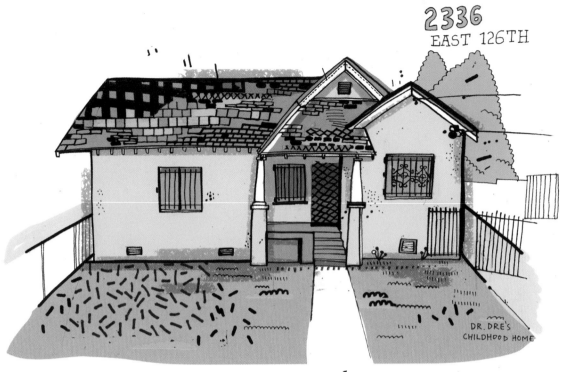

2336
EAST 126TH

DR. DRE'S
CHILDHOOD HOME

INGLEWOOD

RANDY'S DONUTS

805
WEST
MANCHESTER
BOULEVARD

THEME BUILDING AT LAX

OPENED IN 1961

Thanks to all my Los Angeles family. When a city is difficul difficult to integrate into the people that you meet become all the more important: Bianca & Channon, Jessica Koslow, Pat Liem, Sarah Winshall, Chris Thomas, Stella Mosgawa, Erik Kertez. Also to my wife for starting our journey in this crazy city.

Designed and Illustrated by James Gulliver Hancock

First published in the United States of America in 2022 by
Universe Publishing,
A Division of Rizzoli International Publications, Inc.
300 Park Avenue South
New York, NY 10010
www.rizzoliusa.com

Publisher: Charles Miers
Editor: Jessica Fuller
Design: James Gulliver Hancock
Managing Editor: Lynn Scrabis
Production Manager: Colin Hough Trapp

Printed in China

2022 2023 2024 2025 / 10 9 8 7 6 5 4 3 2 1

ISBN: 978-0-7893-3950-8
Library of Congress Control Number: 2020931955